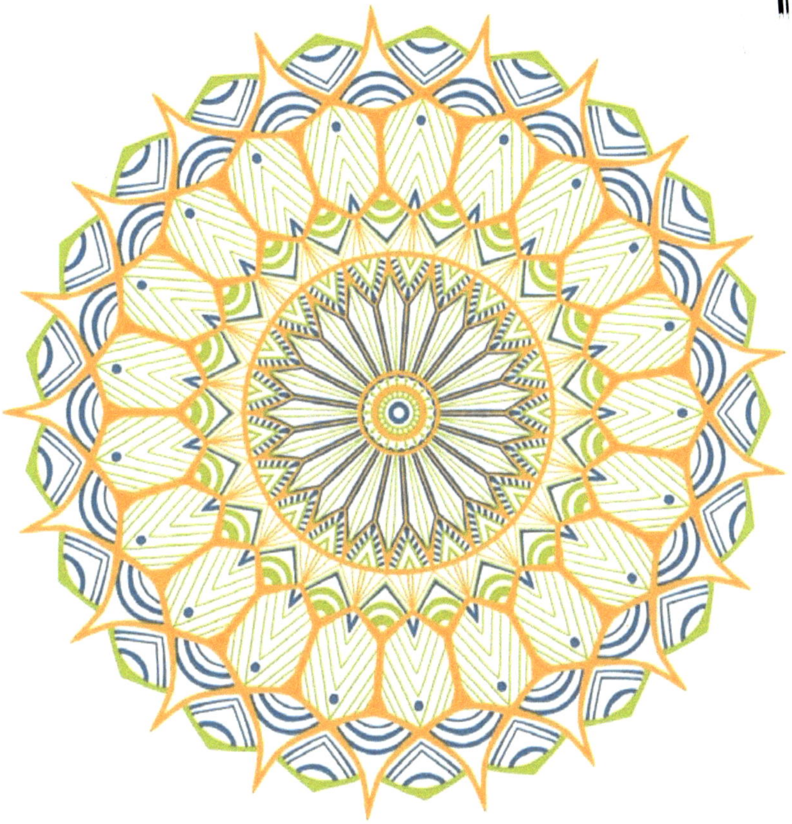

COLORFUL

Coloring book for adult

This book belong to

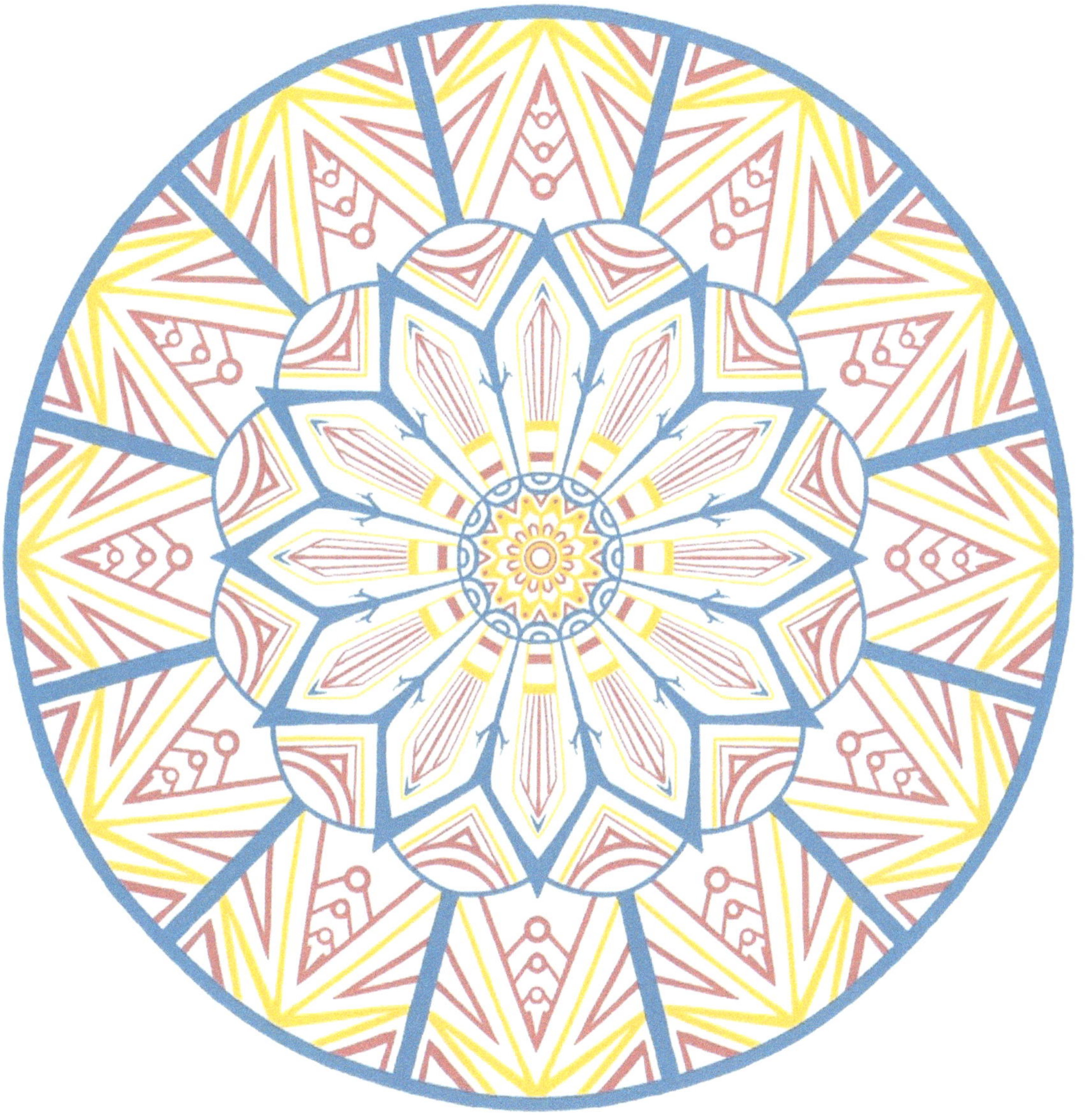

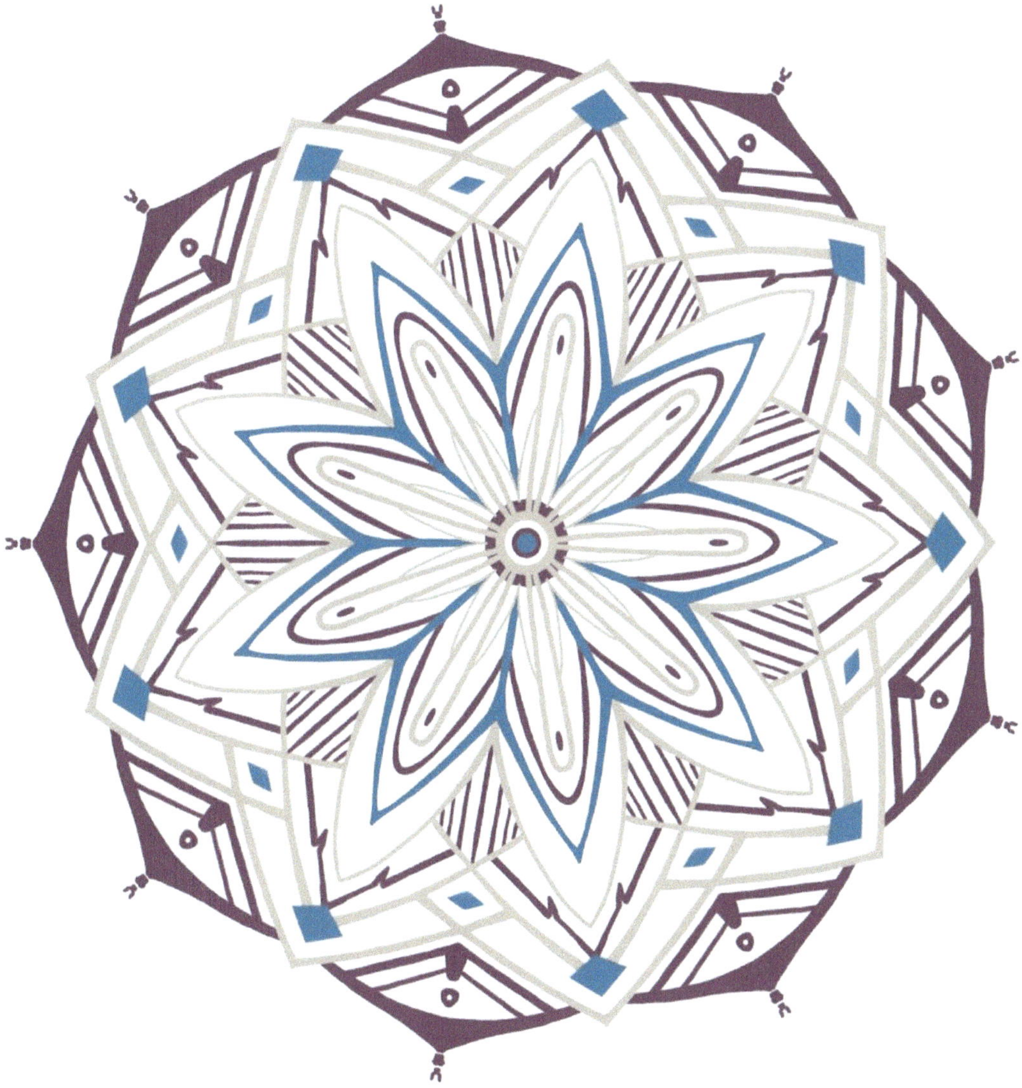

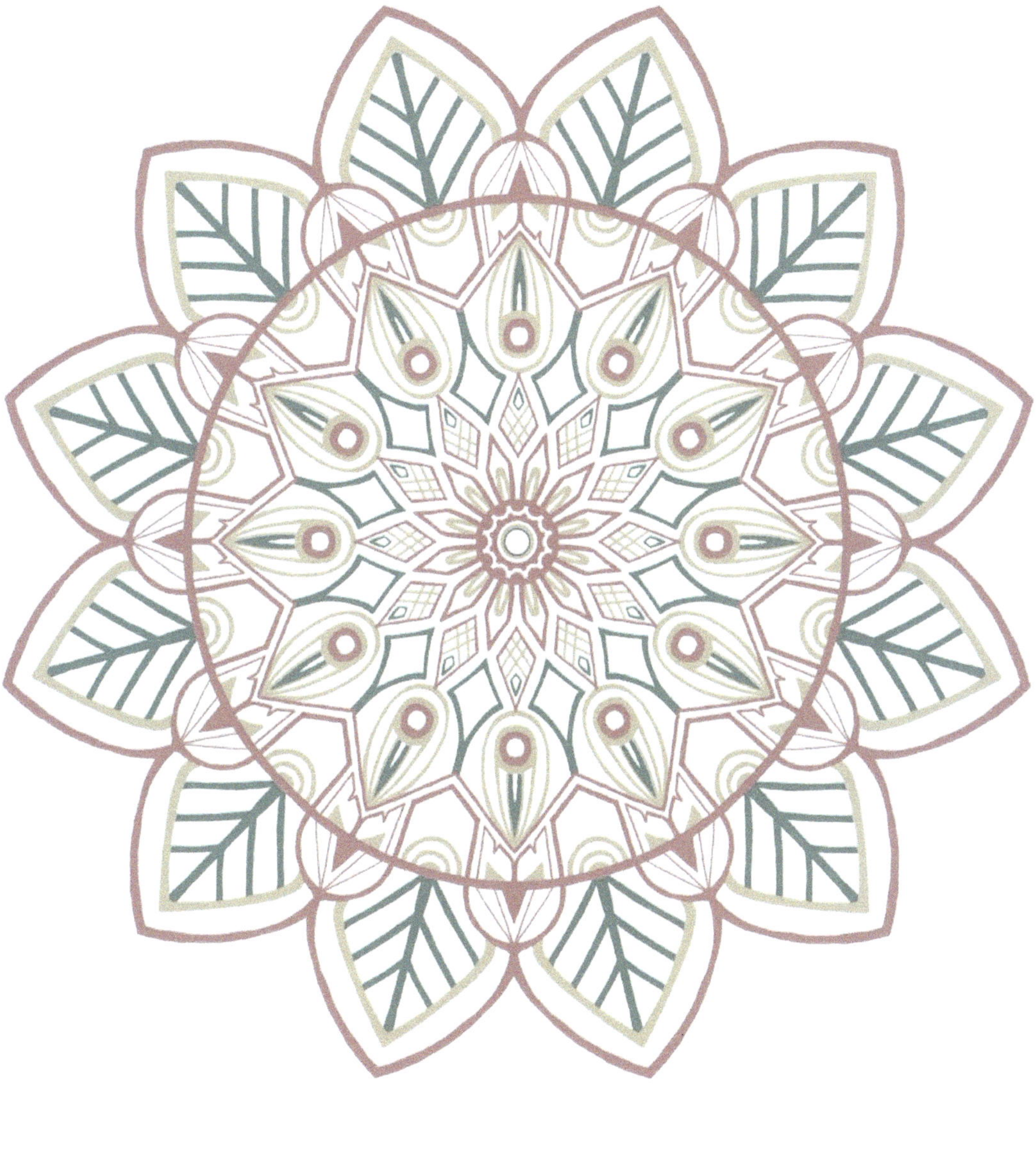

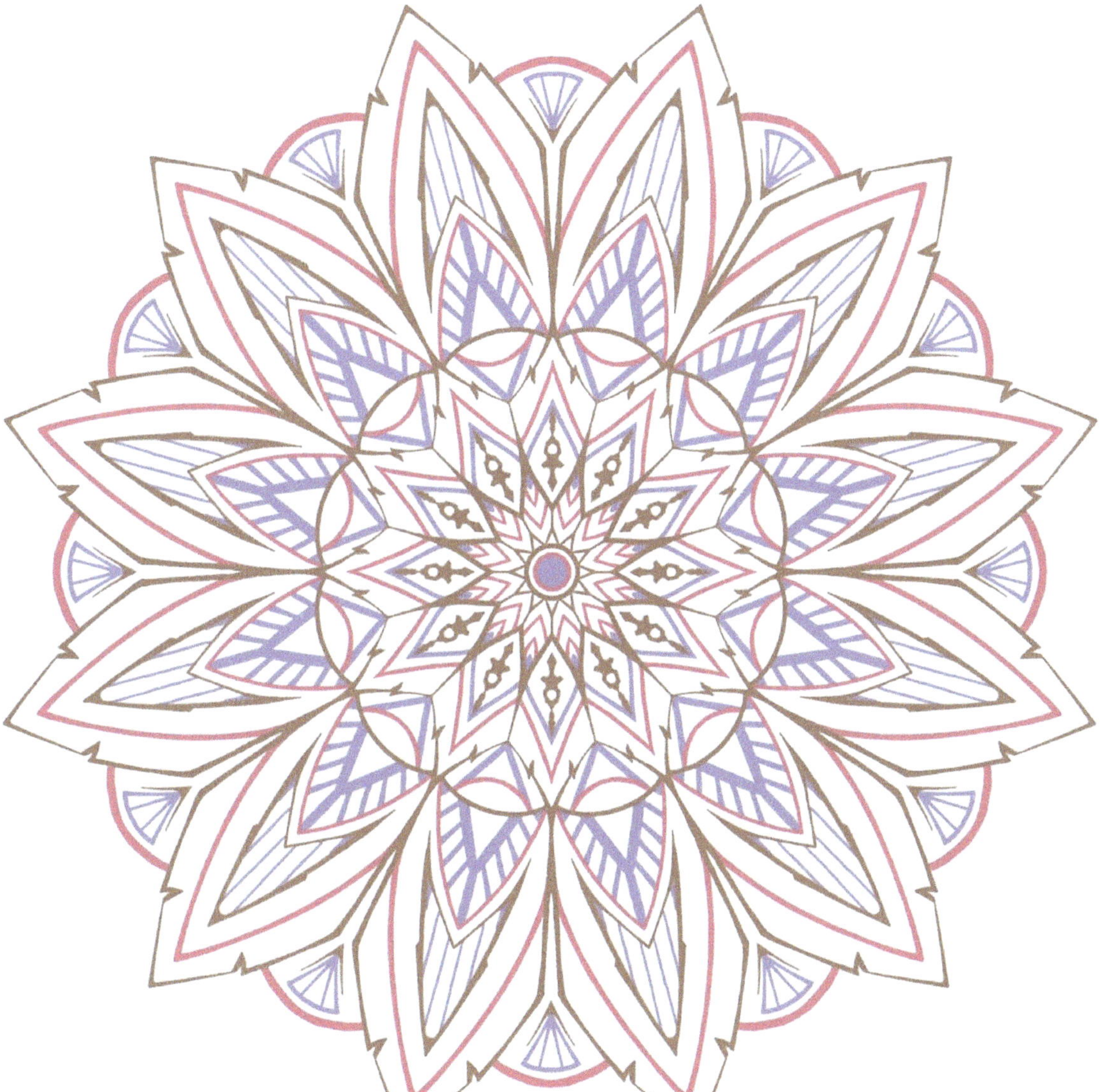

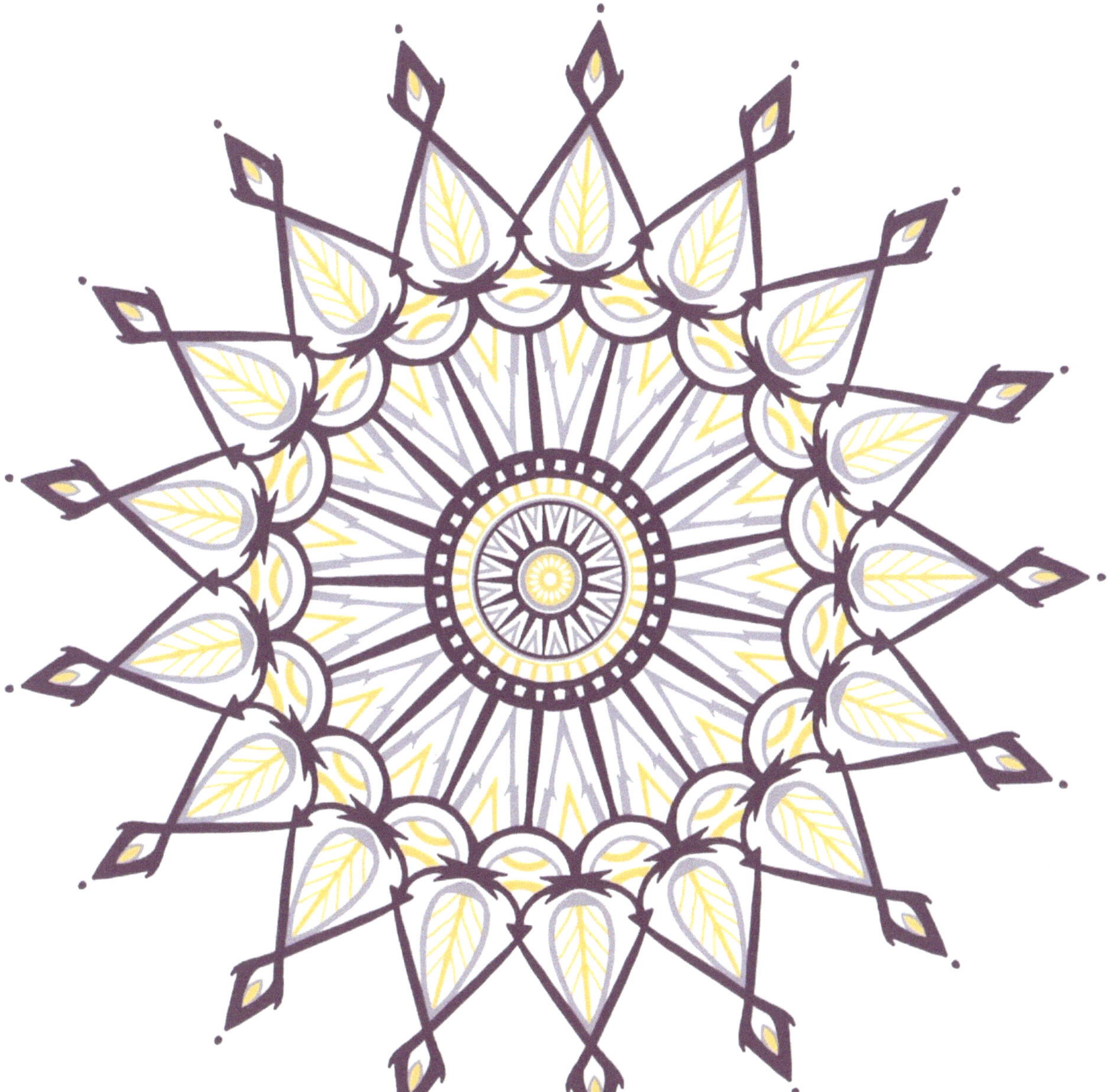

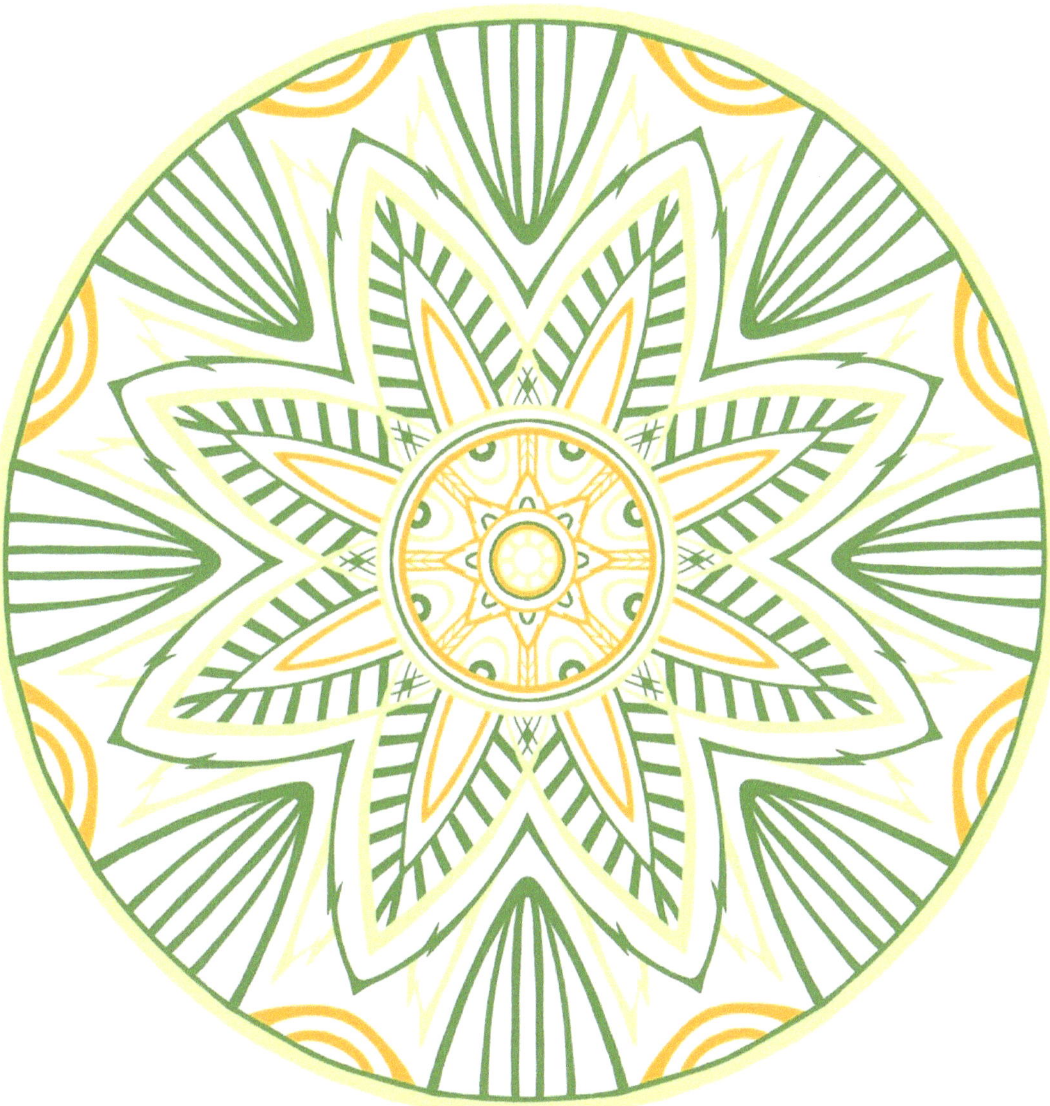

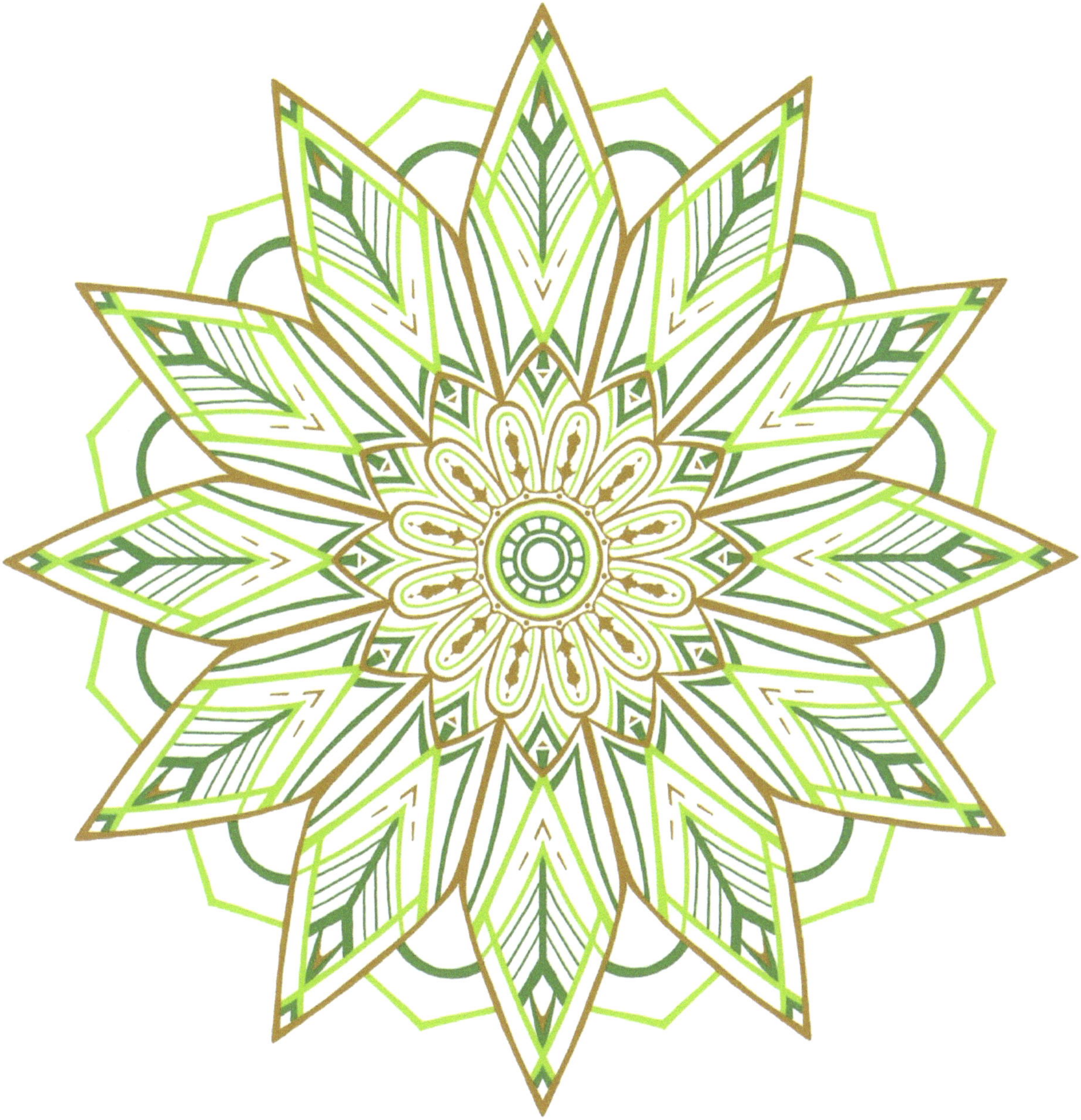

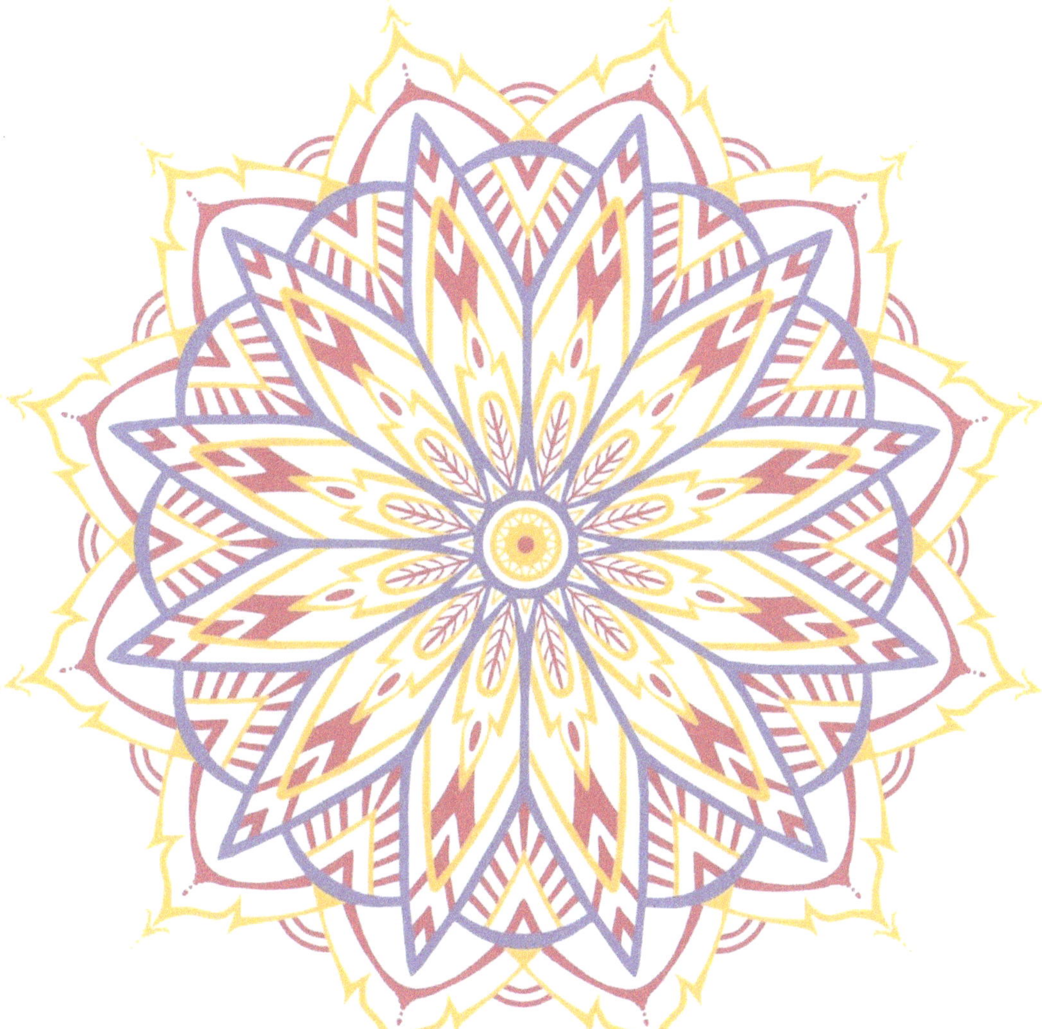

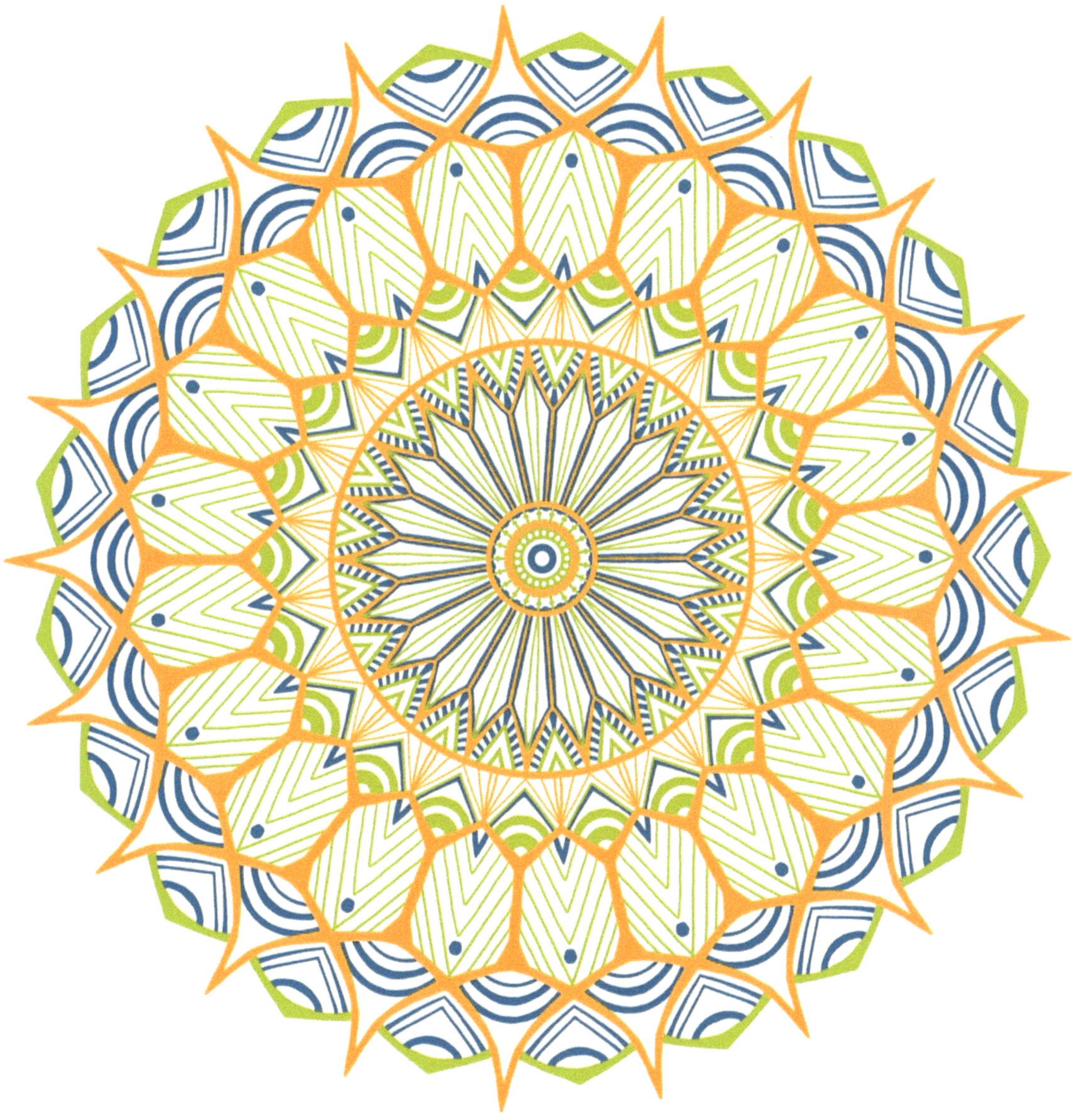

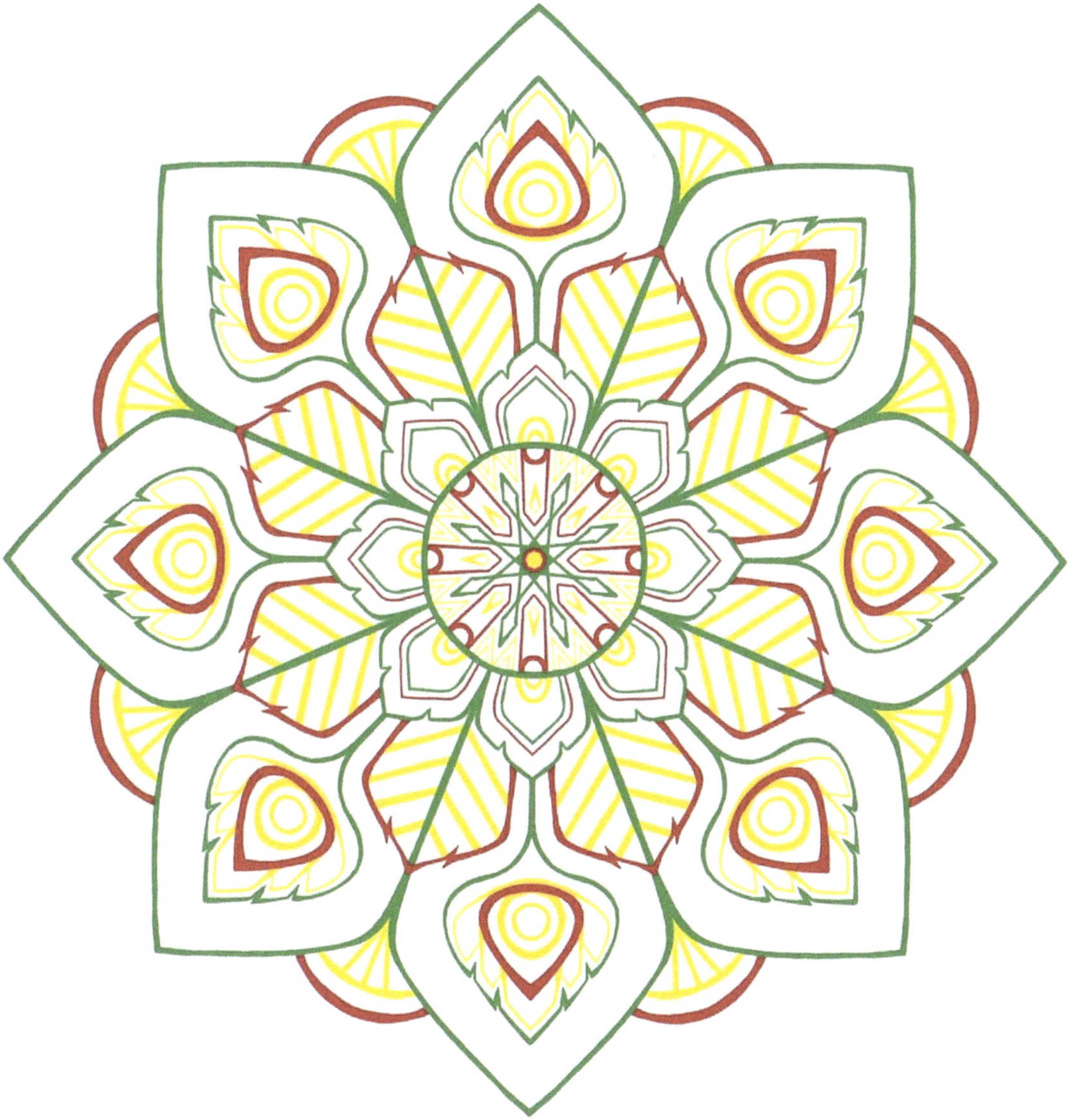

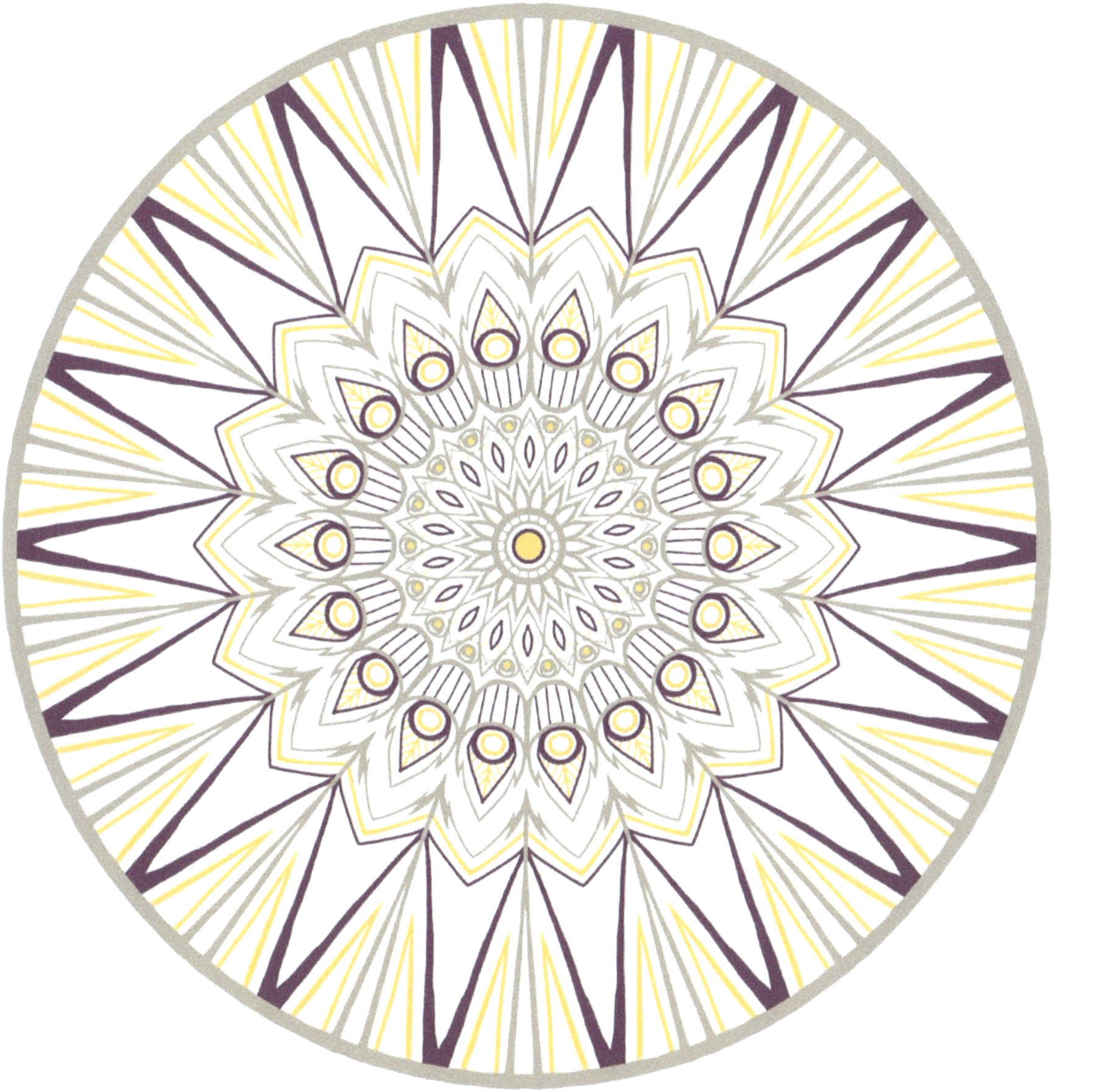

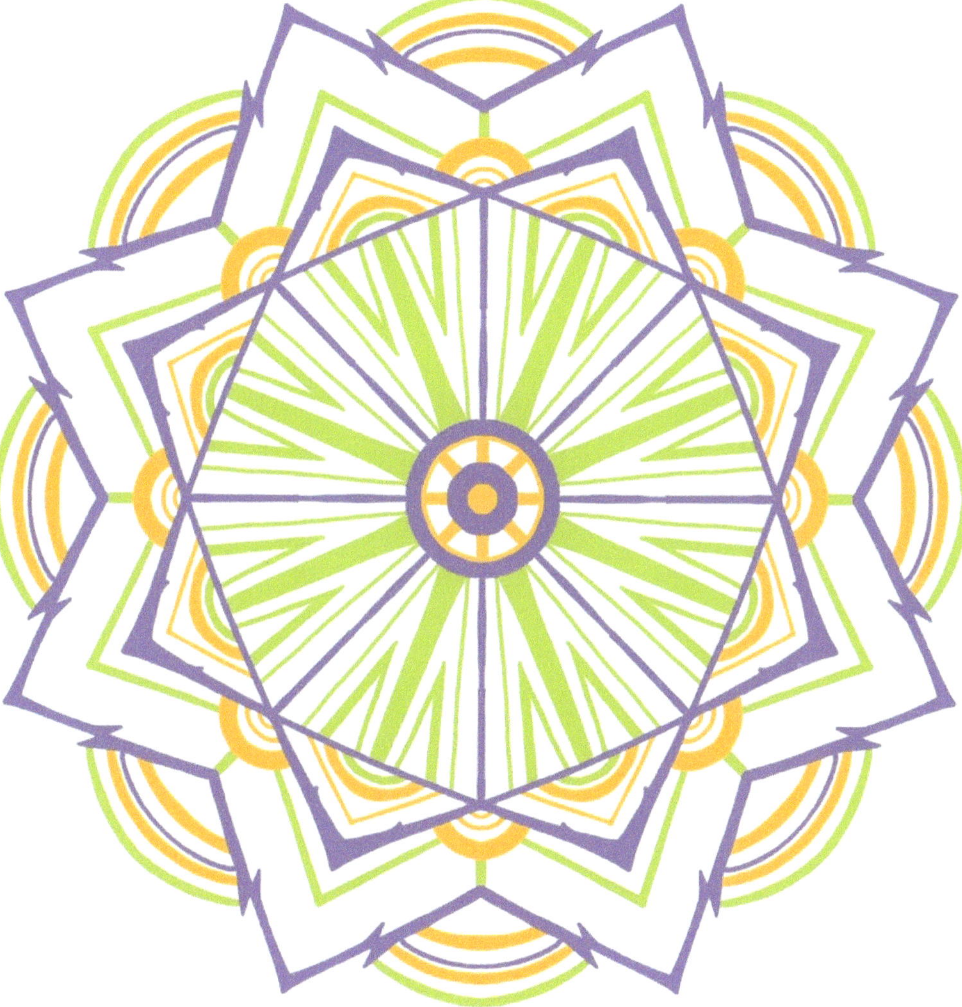

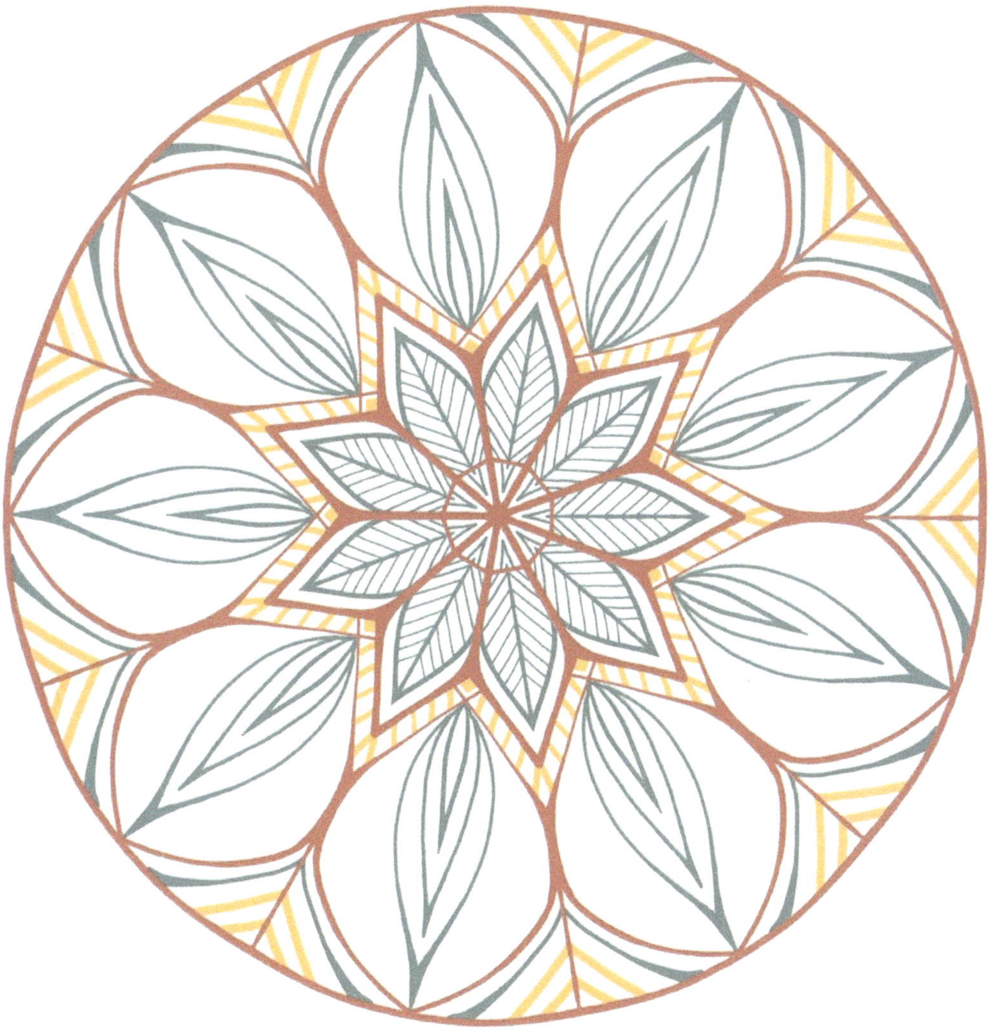

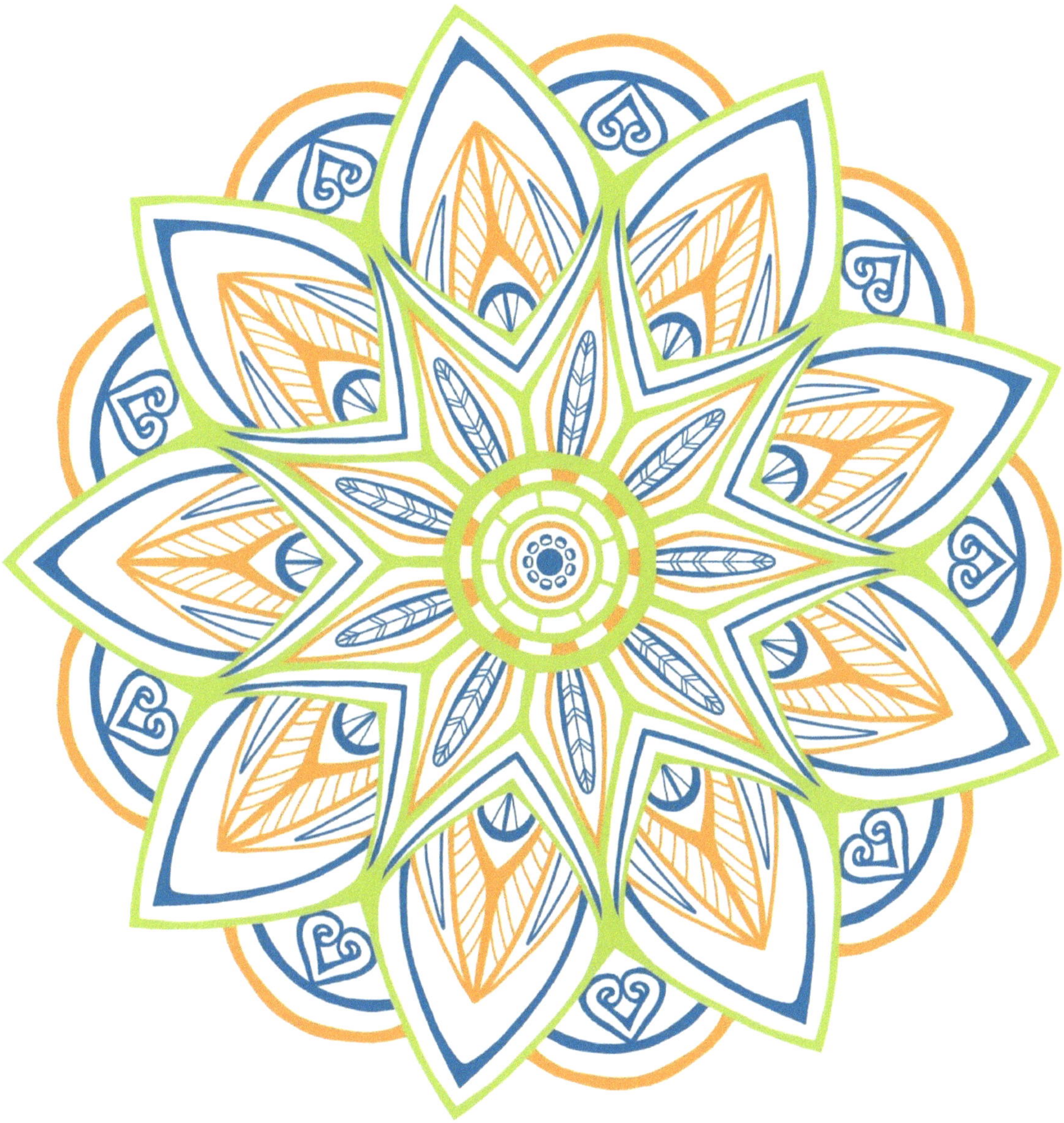

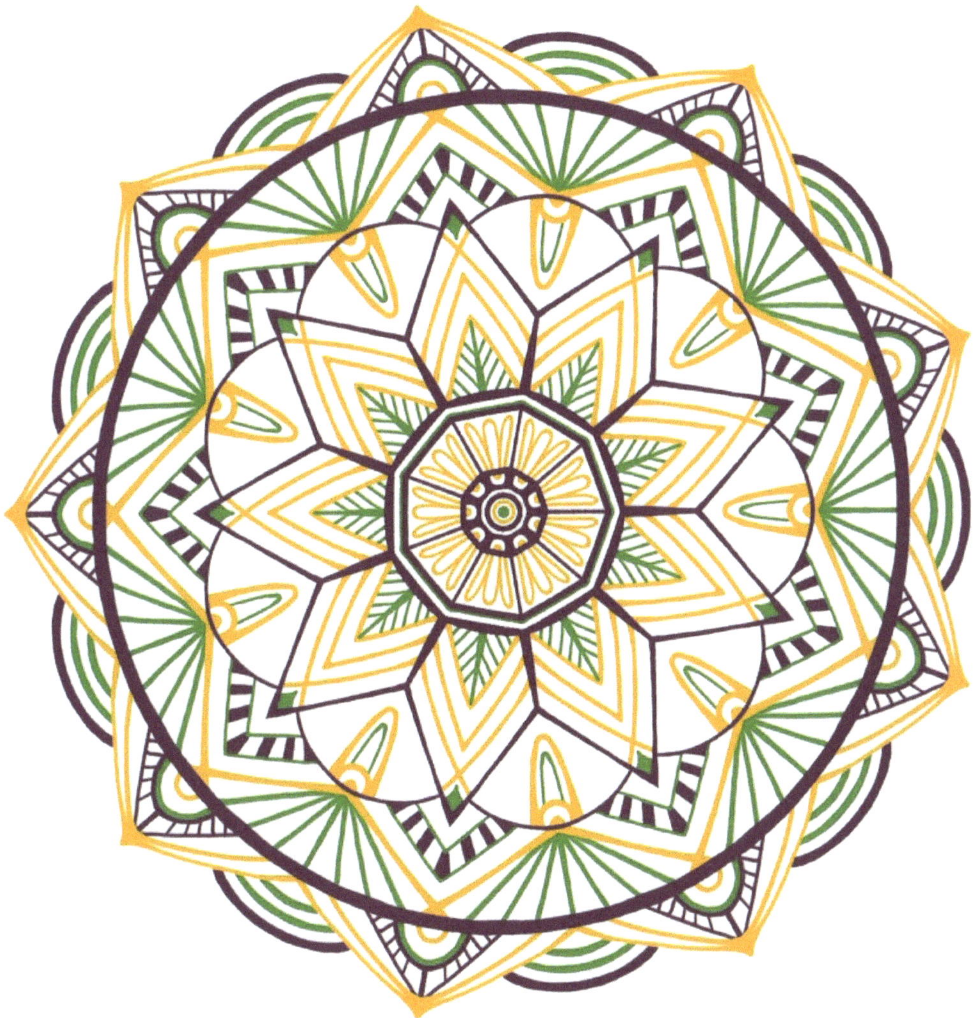

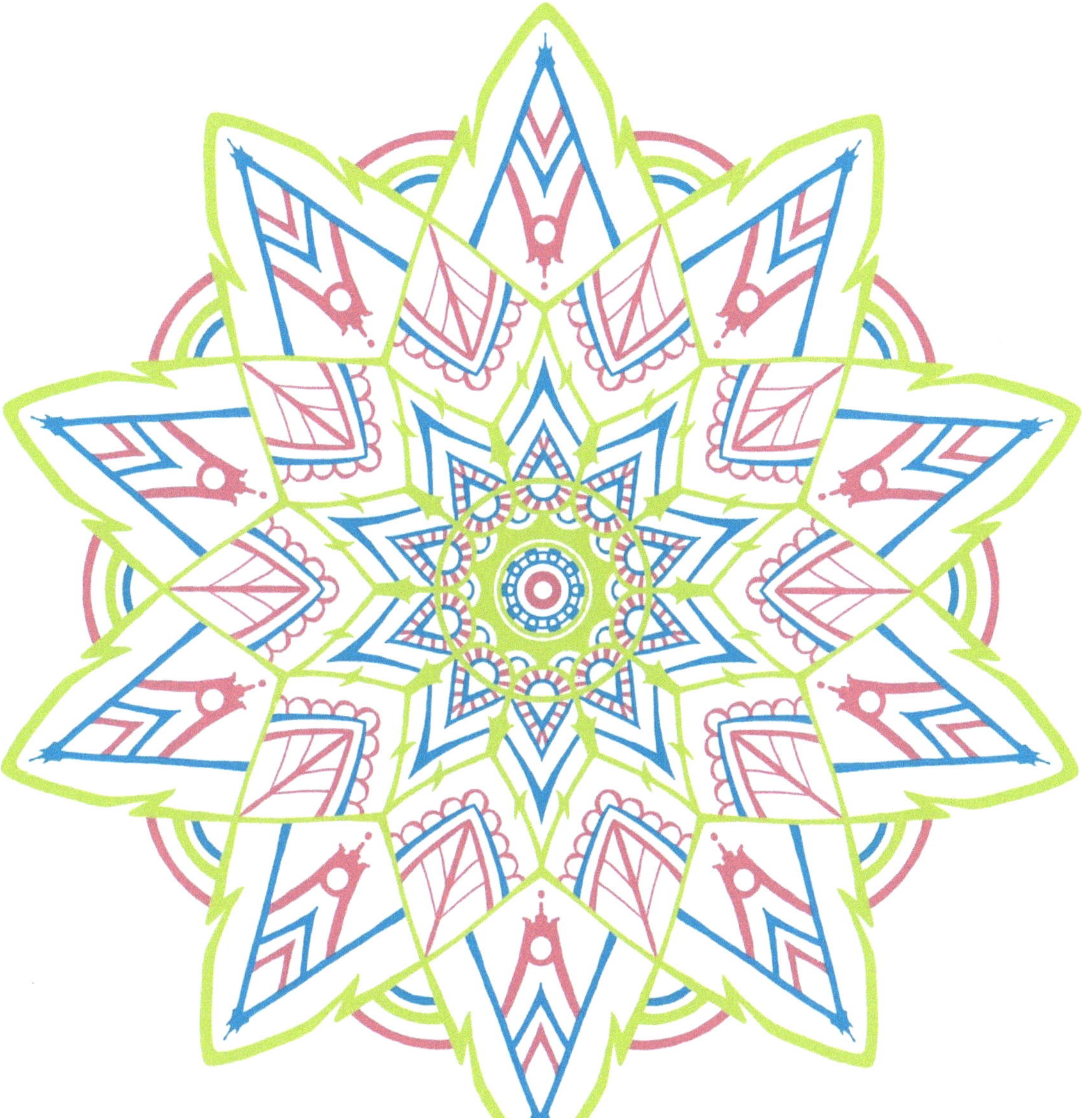

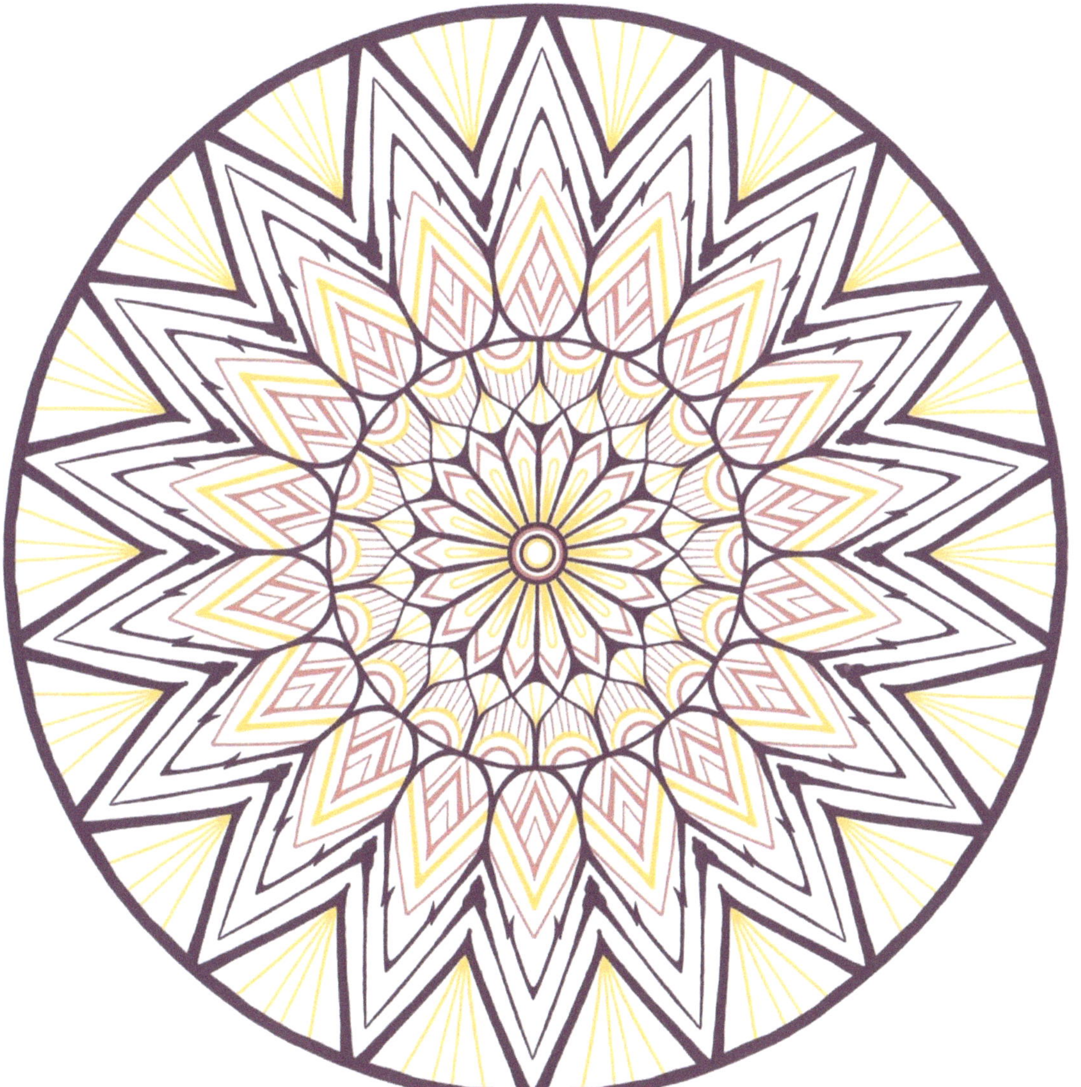

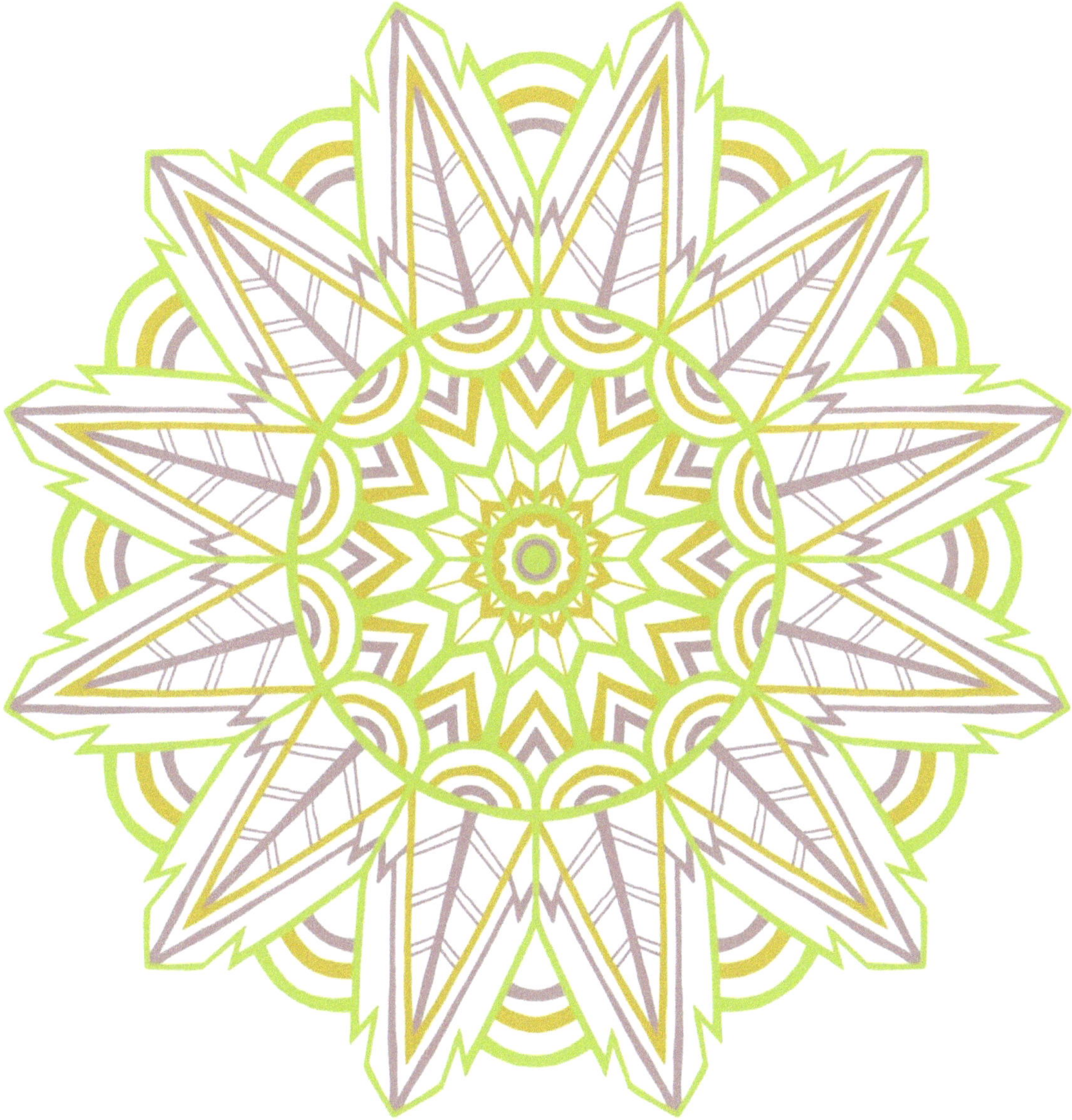

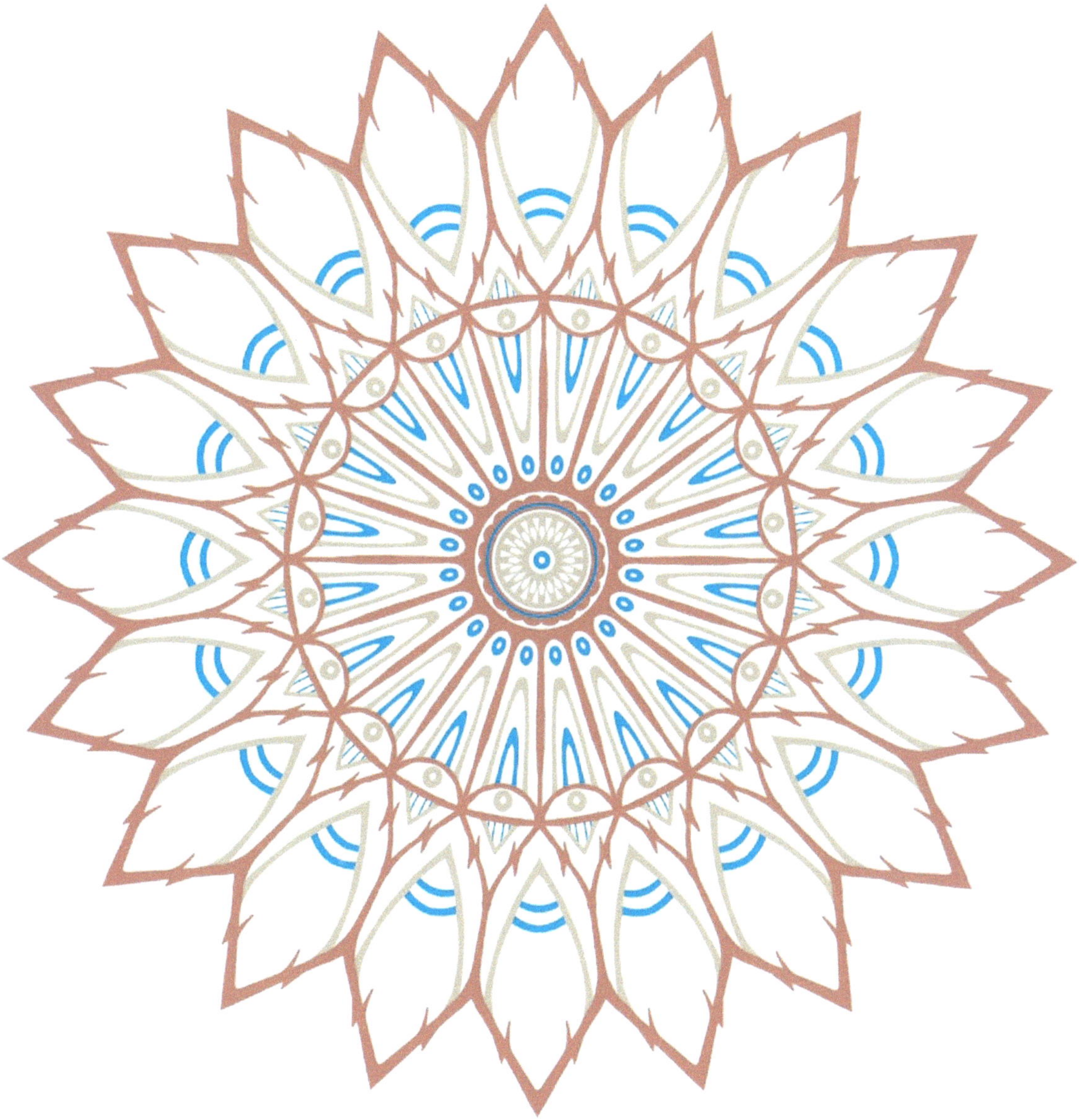

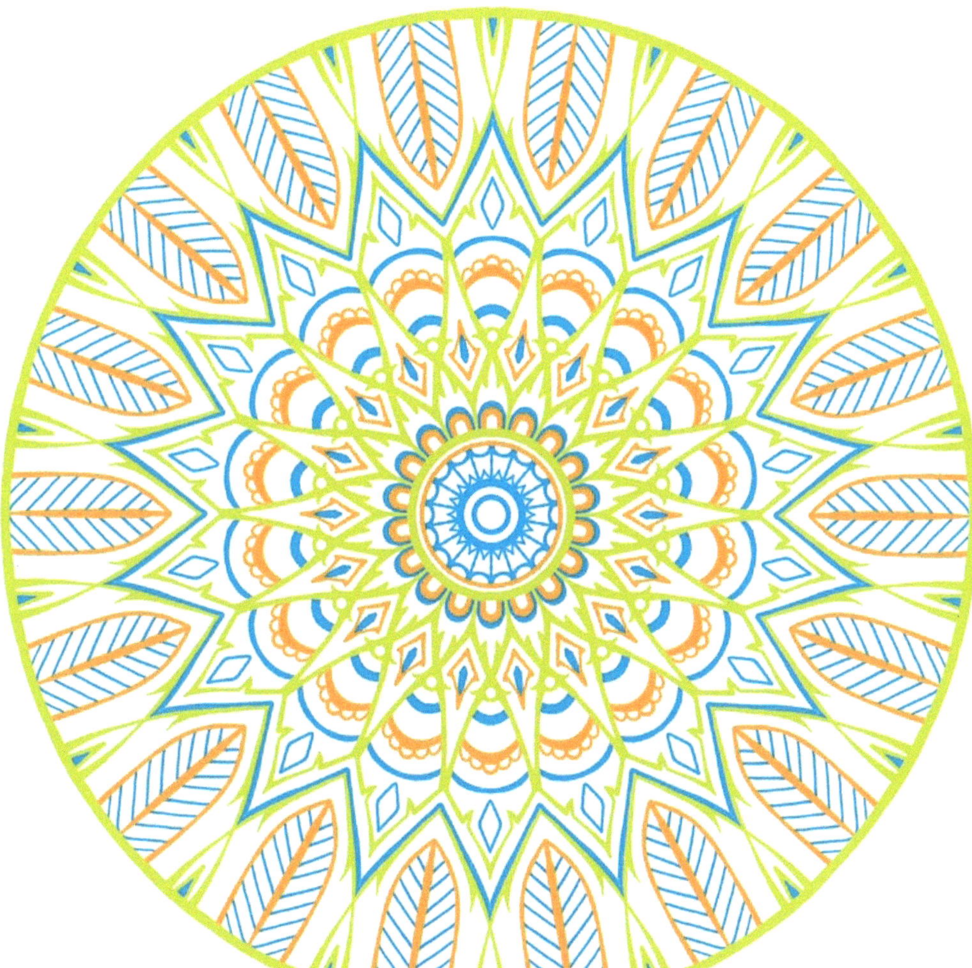

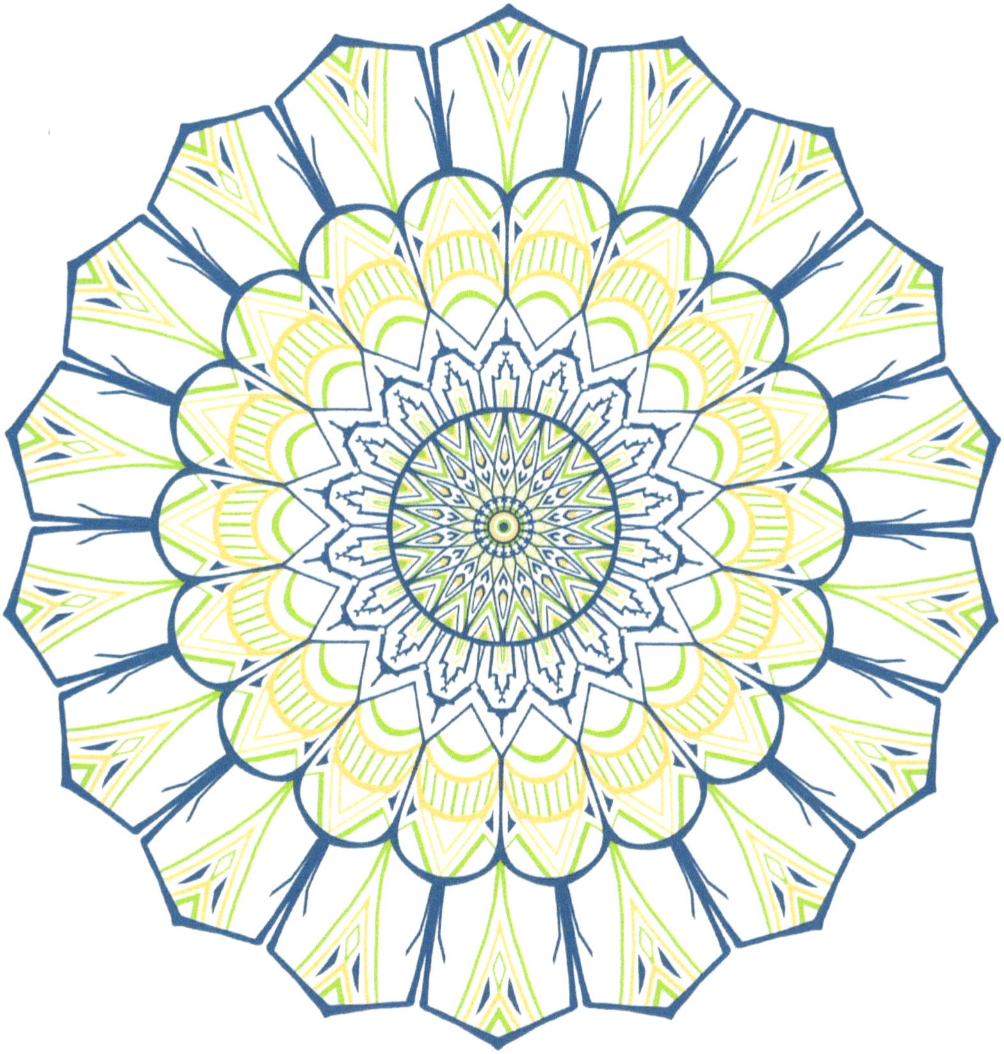

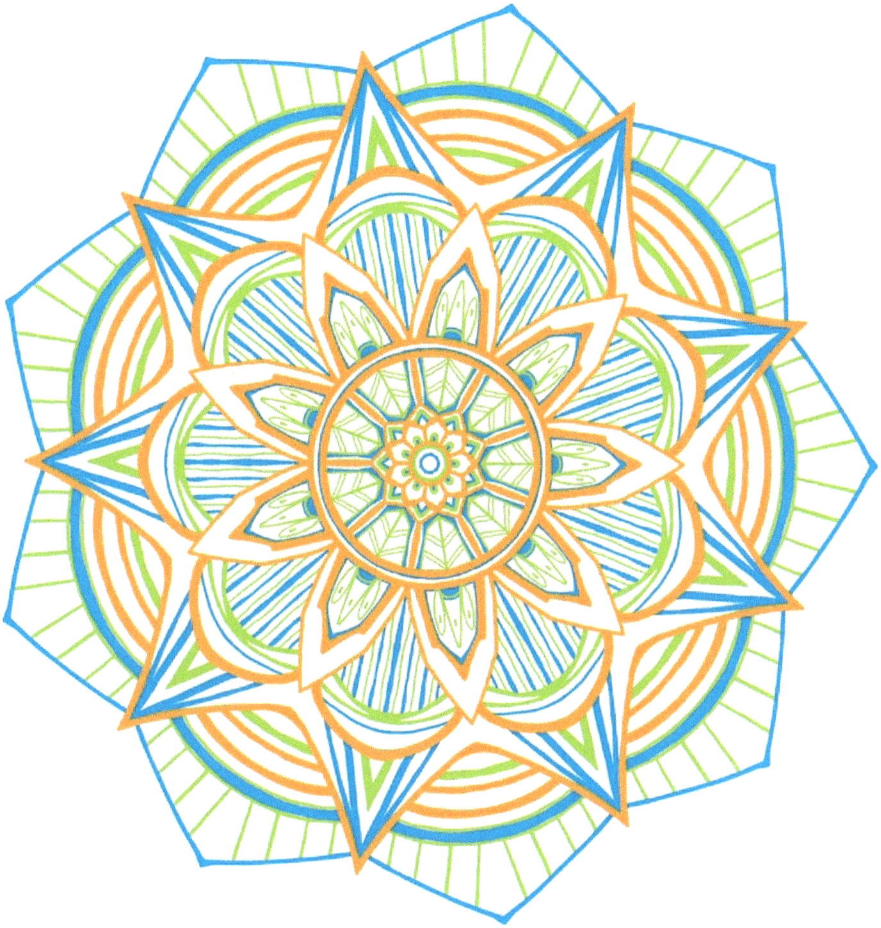

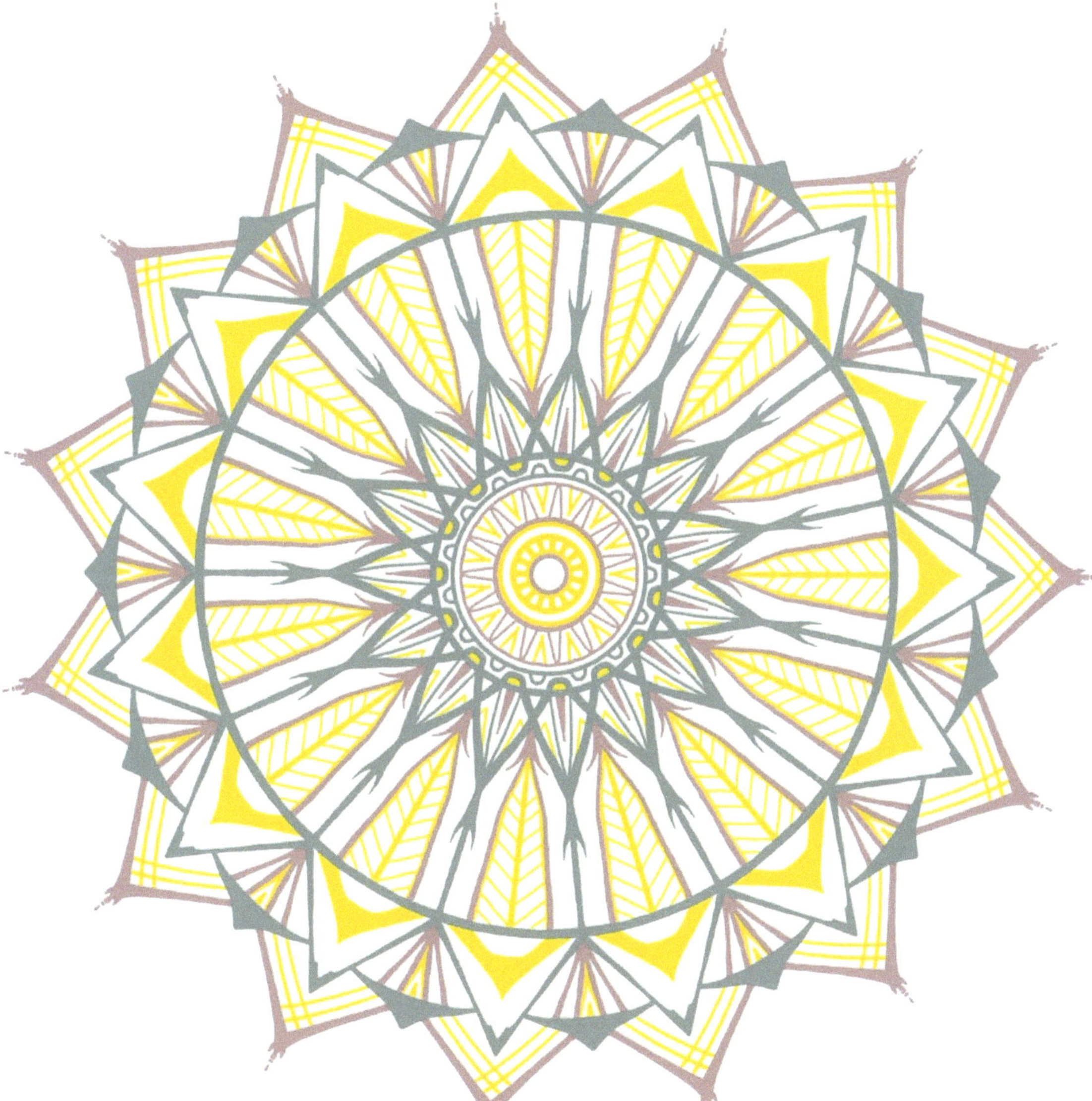

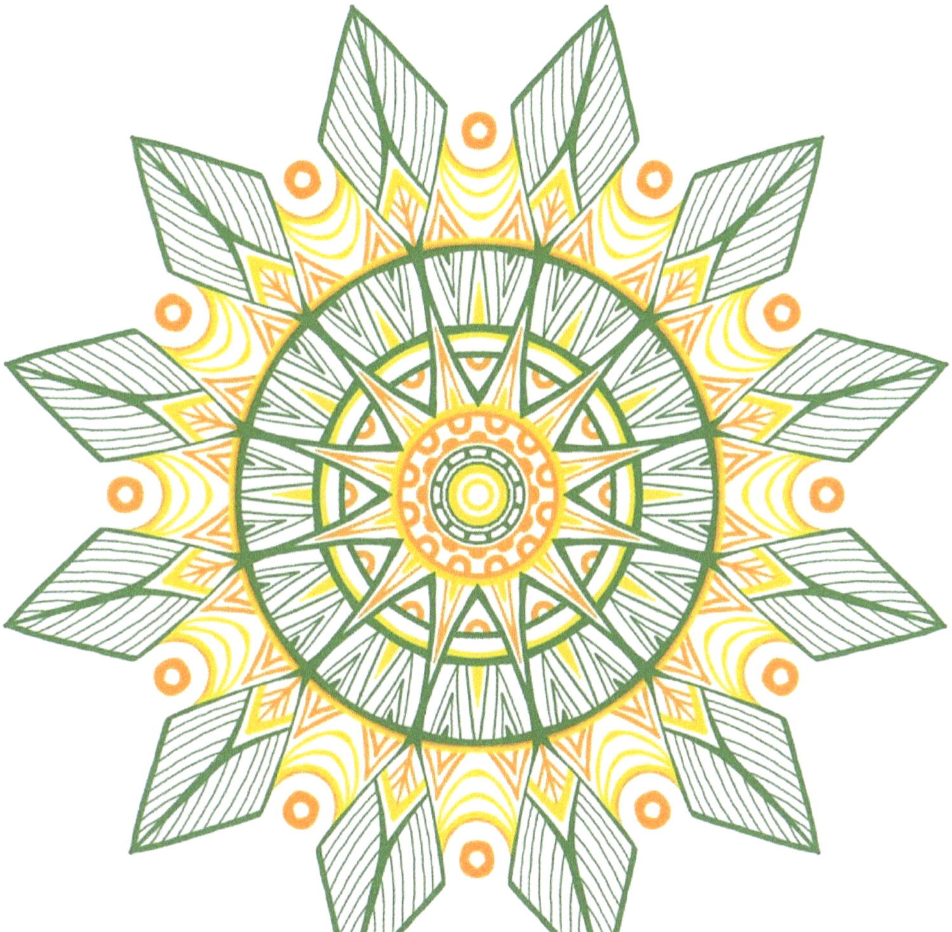

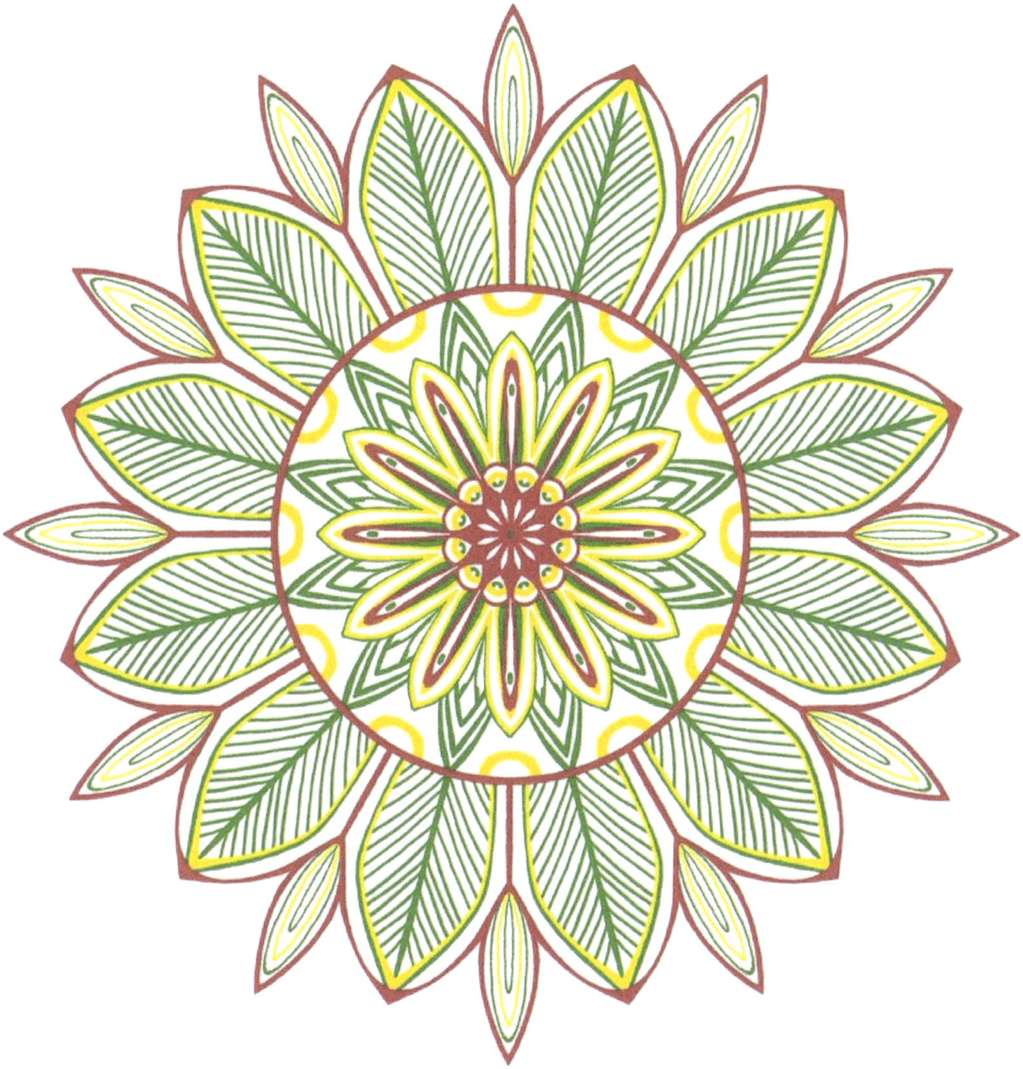

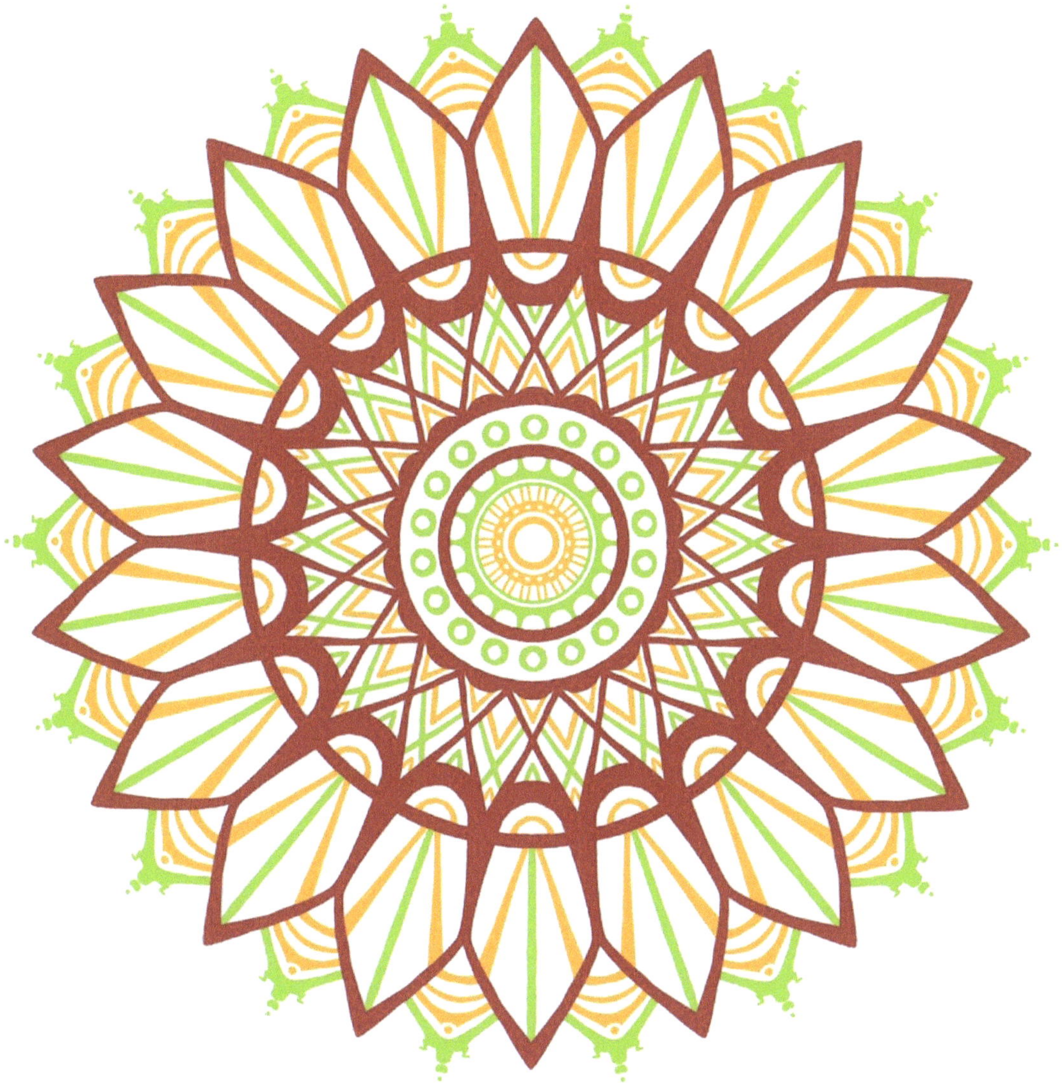

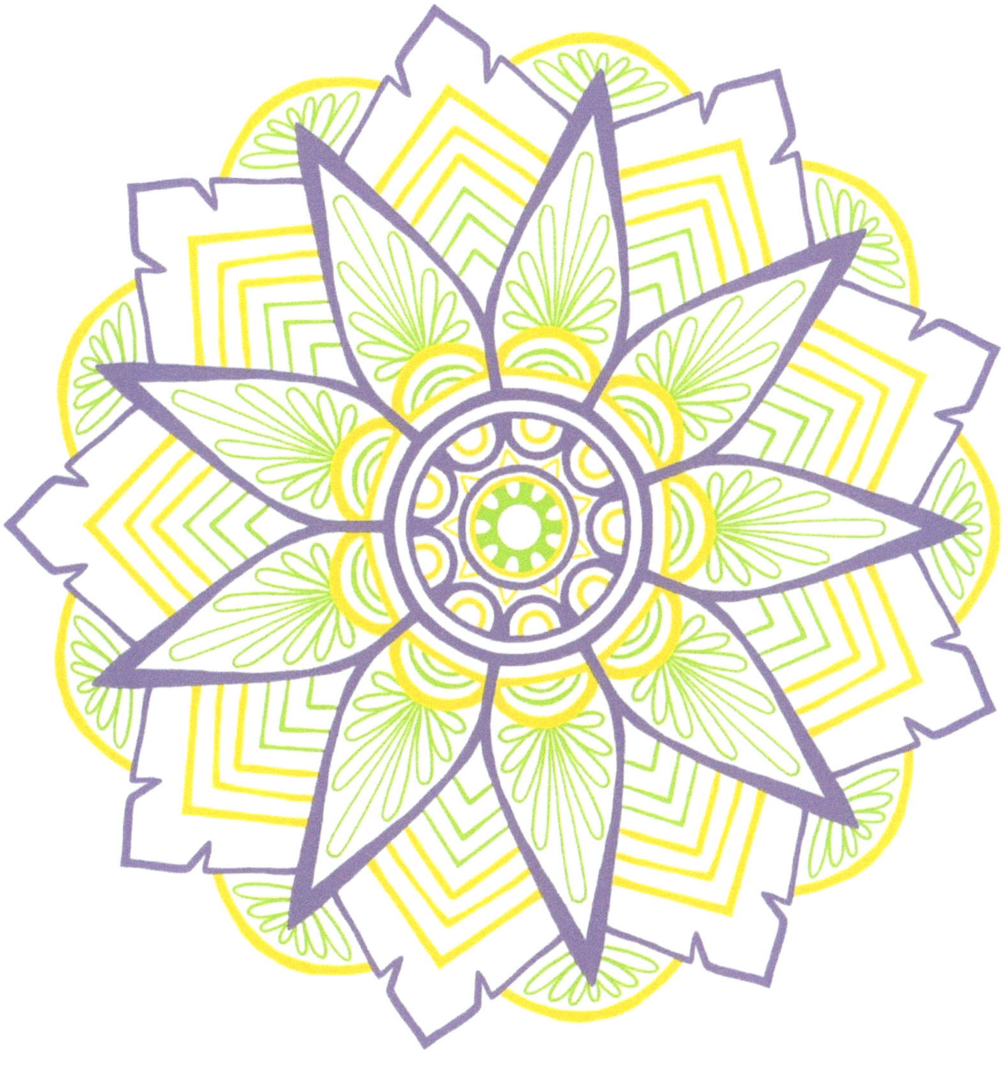

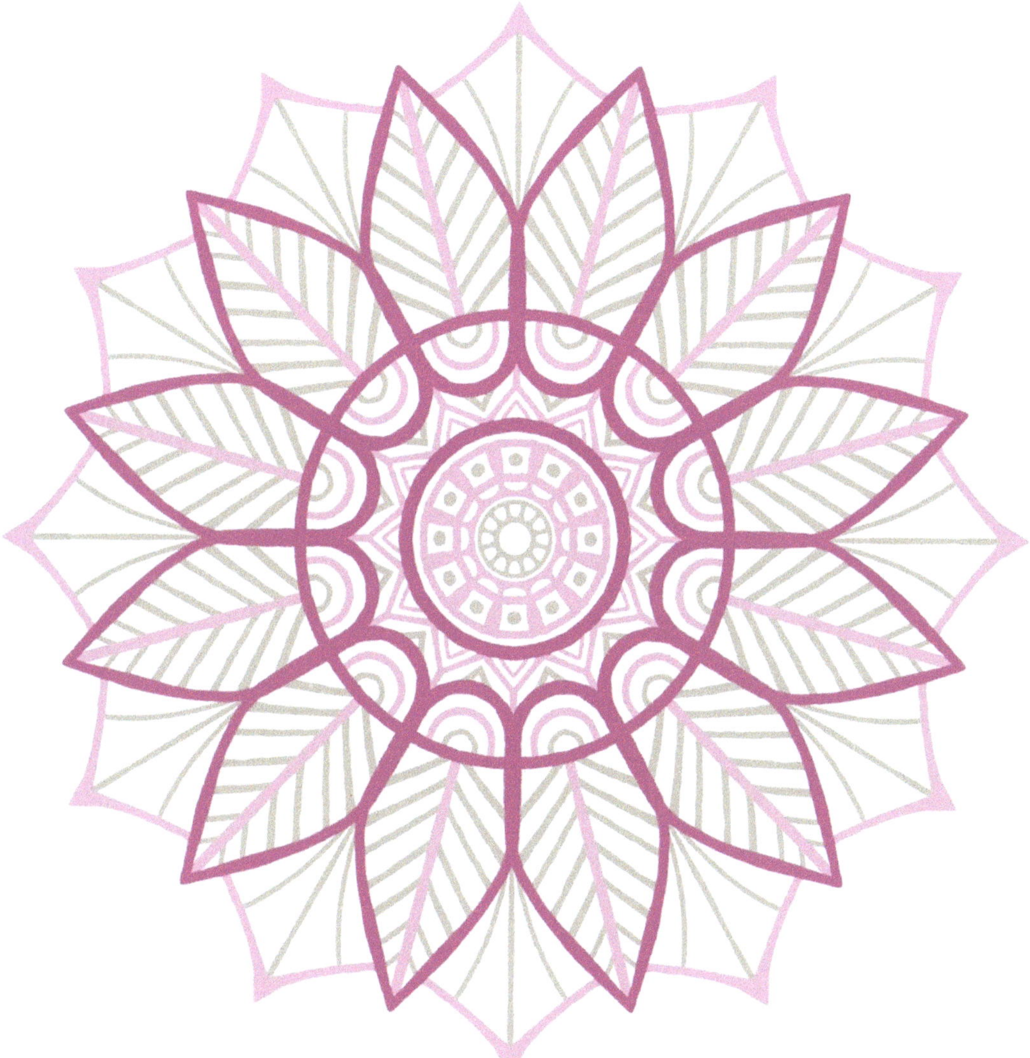

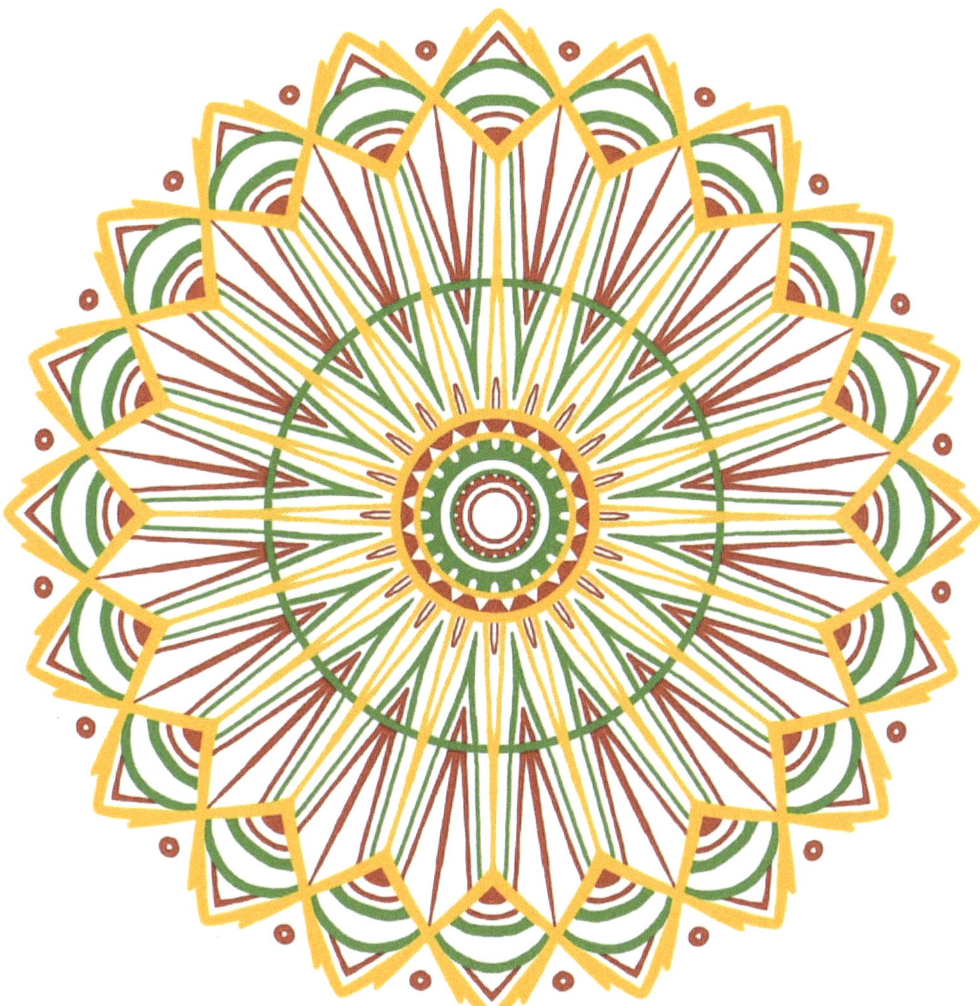

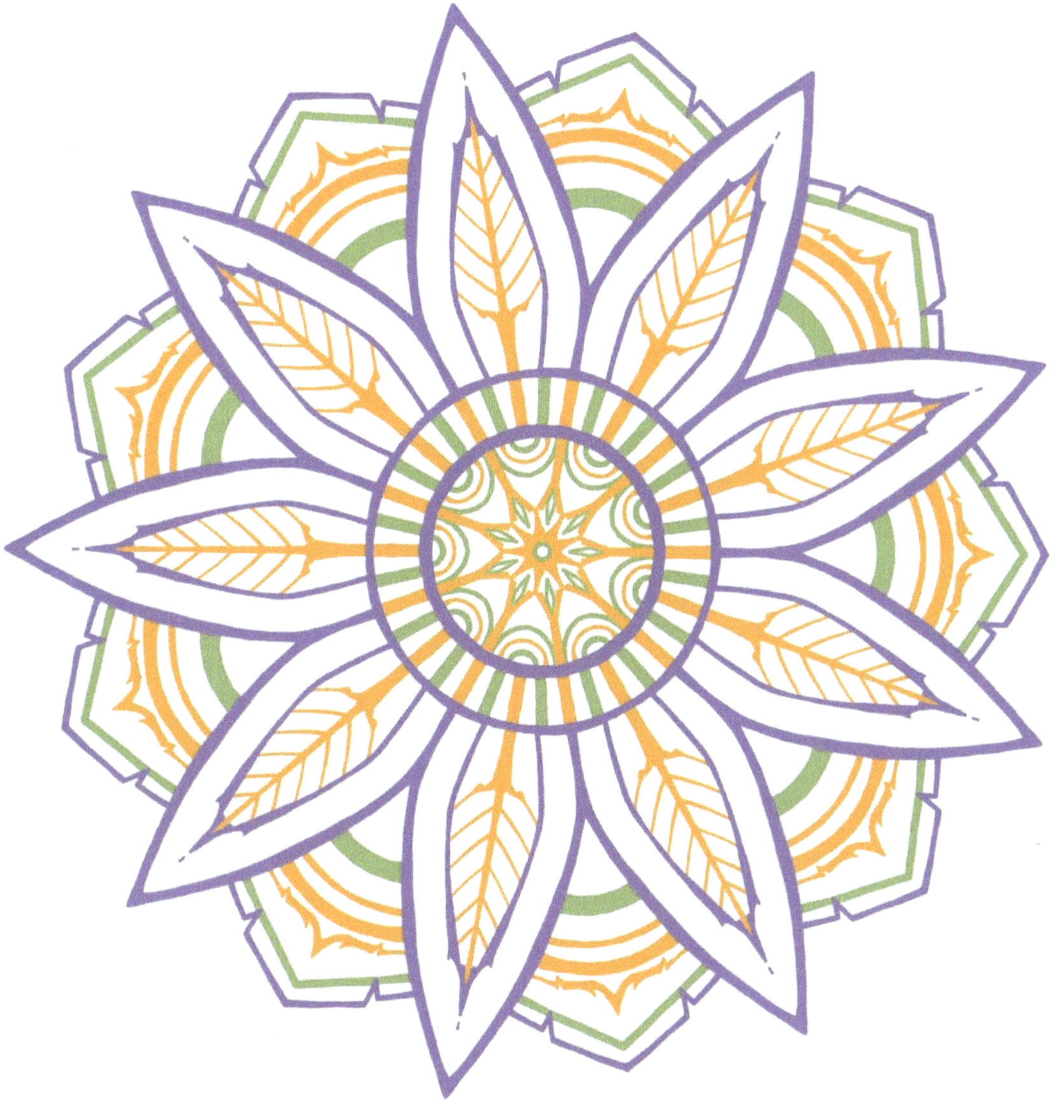

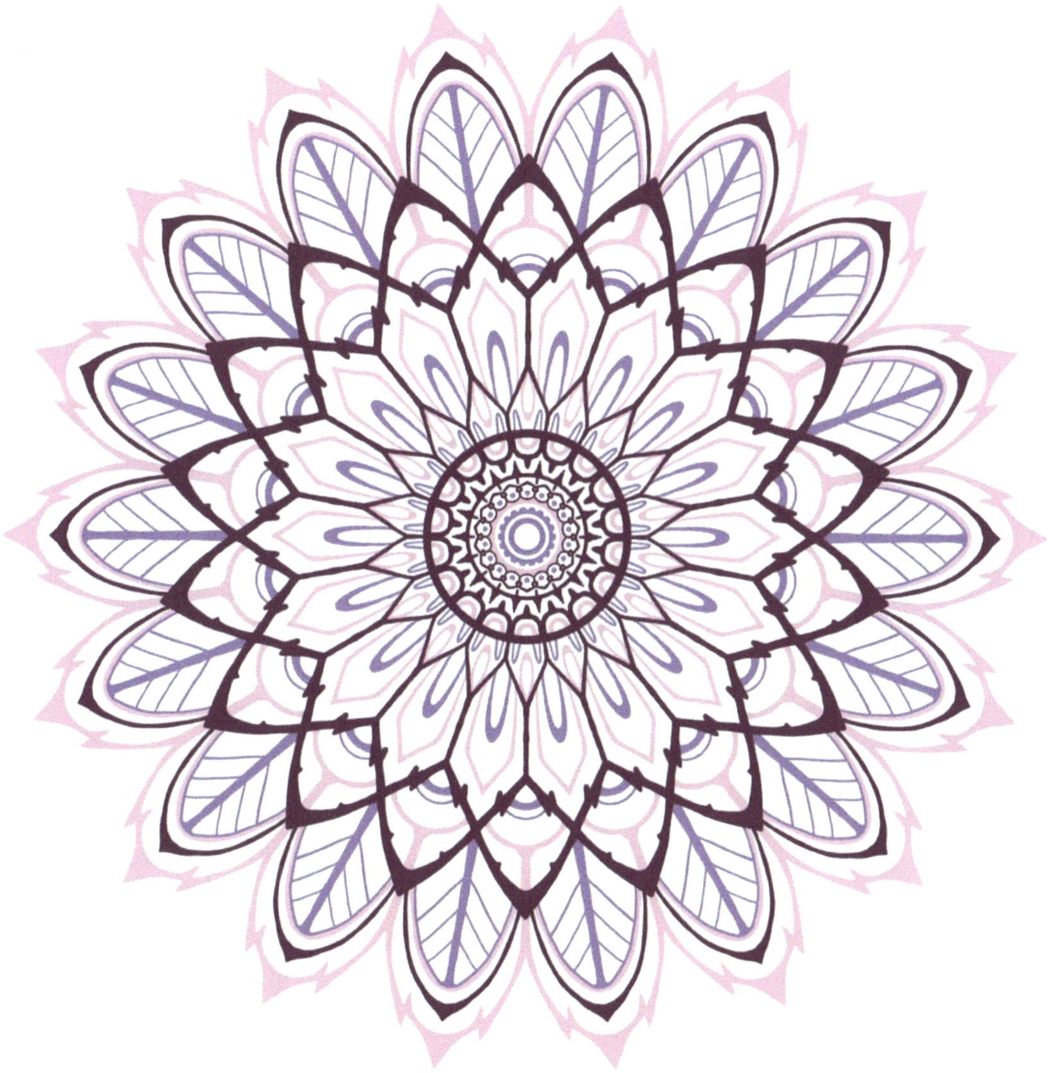

www.ingramcontent.com/pod-product-compliance
Lightning Source LLC
Chambersburg PA
CBHW051206220526
45473CB00003B/923